NICK WOODMAN

Captured Success-The Nick Woodman Story and Rise of GoPro

Ben J. Thompson

All rights reserved. No part of this publication may be reproduced, distributed or transmitted in any form or by any means, including photocopy, recording or other electric or mechanical methods, without the prior written permission of the publisher, except in the case of brief quotations embodied in critical reviews and certain other noncommercial uses permitted by copyright law

Copyright © Ben J. Thompson 2024

CONTENTS

Prologue...5

Chapter One: The Adventurer's Beginnings...8

Chapter Two: From Failure to Fortune..........19

Chapter Three: The Inspiration Behind GoPro..31

Chapter Four: Building from Scratch...........43

Chapter Five: GoPro's Breakthrough............54

Chapter Six: A Brand for Adventurers...........64

Chapter Seven: Innovation and Evolution....75

Chapter Eight:The Power of Social Media....85

Chapter Nine:The Trials of Success..............94

Chapter Ten:Legacy and Lasting Impact....105

Epilogue..115

Acknowledgement......................................118

Prologue

Nick Woodman wasn't born with a silver spoon. He wasn't groomed to lead a billion-dollar empire or destined to become one of Silicon Valley's most daring innovators. He was, first and foremost, a surfer, an adventurer, a guy chasing the next thrill. But, like all dreamers who are willing to throw themselves wholeheartedly into the unknown, Nick Woodman had a spark—one that would ignite a revolution.

In the late 1990s, Nick tasted failure firsthand. His first startup crumbled, leaving him to wrestle with disappointment, self-doubt, and a pressing question: what do you do when your greatest effort just isn't enough? For most, that might have been the end of the road, but for Nick, it was the beginning of a story no one could have predicted. He was broke, but not beaten. It was during a soul-searching trip to Australia, where he sought escape in the waves, that an idea took root in his mind. What if he could find a way to capture moments of exhilaration—moments that truly meant something—without needing someone else behind the camera?And so, with nothing but grit and a relentless drive to create, Nick would build something extraordinary from the ground up: GoPro, a brand that would forever change the way we capture life's moments.But the journey wasn't straightforward. GoPro wasn't just a stroke of luck; it was the product of Nick's restless vision, his willingness to embrace failure, and his talent for harnessing the thrill-seeker within us all. GoPro would go on to capture moments around the world—from surfers conquering massive waves to astronauts floating in space. Yet, behind every powerful shot was the story of one man who dared to turn his dreams into reality, one lens at a time.

This book isn't just about Nick Woodman or the brand he built. It's about the spirit of invention, the value of resilience, and the extraordinary power of a simple idea. Here begins the story of Nick Woodman's captured success.

1

The Adventurer's Beginnings

Long before GoPro cameras captured extreme sports enthusiasts hurling themselves off cliffs or surfers riding monster waves, a young boy stood in his California backyard, dreaming of adventures that would one day change how we document our most thrilling moments. Nick Woodman wasn't born with a silver spoon or destined for guaranteed success – instead, he was blessed with something far more valuable: an insatiable appetite for life and an imagination that refused to be tamed.

Born in 1975 to Concepcion and Dean Woodman in Atherton, California, Nick grew up in a household that valued both education and entrepreneurship. His father, an investment banker who brought Volkswagen to America, provided an early glimpse into the world of business. However, it wasn't the boardrooms or balance sheets that captured young Nick's attention – it was the allure of the great outdoors and the thrill of pushing boundaries.As a child, Nick was anything but ordinary. While other kids were content playing video games, he could be found constructing elaborate ramps for his bike, much to his mother's mixture of pride and concern. "I was always that kid who had to take things one step further," Woodman would later recall in interviews. "If someone jumped their bike over one trash can, I had to try two. It wasn't about showing off – it was about discovering what was possible."

This early appetite for pushing limits wasn't limited to physical adventures. Nick's entrepreneurial spirit emerged early, manifesting in creative ways that hinted at his future success. At age 10, he started his first "business" selling seashells he collected from the beach, carefully arranging them on his wagon and wheeling them around the neighborhood. While the venture might not have made him rich, it planted the seeds of understanding the connection between passion and profit.High school brought new adventures and challenges. At Menlo School, an elite private institution in Atherton, Nick wasn't the typical straight-A student. Instead, he was the kid who always had a new idea, a fresh perspective, or a wild plan brewing. His teachers often noted his unique ability to think differently, even if his attention sometimes wandered from traditional academics to more exciting pursuits.It was during these teenage years that Nick discovered his first true love: surfing. The moment he caught his first wave at Half Moon Bay, something clicked. The combination of physical challenge, natural beauty, and the pure rush of riding a wave awakened something in him. Surfing wasn't just a hobby – it became a lens through which he viewed life's possibilities. The sport taught him patience, persistence, and the art of reading situations and adapting quickly – skills that would prove invaluable in his future endeavors.

"Surfing changed everything for me," Woodman would later explain. "It taught me that the best things in life require work, timing, and the courage to paddle out even when the waves look intimidating.

Sometimes you wipe out, but that's part of the journey."

His passion for surfing led to another discovery: photography. Frustrated by the inability to capture his surfing adventures, Nick began experimenting with different ways to document his experiences. This combination of interests – adventure sports and visual documentation – would later become the foundation of his greatest innovation, though he didn't know it yet.

College years at the University of California, San Diego, expanded Nick's horizons further. While pursuing a degree in visual arts and creative writing, he became known as the campus entrepreneur. Between classes, he could be found brainstorming business ideas or planning his next surfing trip. His college roommates remember him as someone who never seemed to sleep, always buzzing with energy and new ideas.

It was during this time that Nick's creative and business instincts began to merge. He joined the UCSD Waterski team, serving as team president and learning valuable lessons about leadership and organization. More importantly, he continued to feed his addiction to adrenaline-pumping activities, adding skiing, mountain biking, and racing to his repertoire of adventures.But perhaps the most significant development during his college years was the refinement of his problem-solving mindset. Whether it was figuring out how to balance his studies with his adventures or finding creative ways to fund his surfing trips, Nick developed a knack for turning challenges into opportunities. This ability to see solutions where others saw obstacles would become his trademark in the business world.

One particular incident during his junior year perfectly encapsulated the essence of who Nick was becoming. During a surfing trip to Indonesia, he found himself frustrated by the inability to capture his experiences in a way that truly conveyed the excitement and energy of the moment. Traditional cameras were too bulky and risky to use in the water, and hiring photographers was too expensive for a college student. This frustration planted a seed in his mind – one that would later grow into a revolutionary idea.

As graduation approached in 1997, Nick wasn't focused on traditional career paths. While his classmates were sending out resumes to corporate recruiters, he was sketching ideas in notebooks and dreaming up ways to combine his passions into a sustainable future. He had developed a clear understanding of who he was: an adventurer at heart, an entrepreneur in spirit, and someone who refused to accept the limitations of conventional thinking.The energy and optimism of his college years, however, were about to meet the harsh realities of the business world. As the 1990s drew to a close, Nick would face challenges that would test his resilience and determination in ways he never imagined. But these challenges would also forge the character and determination needed for his future success.

Nick's early years laid the foundation for everything that would follow. His childhood creativity, teenage adventures, and college experiences all contributed to forming a unique perspective on life and business. He learned that the best ideas come from solving real problems, that passion can fuel persistence, and that sometimes the biggest risks lead to the greatest rewards.

Looking back at these formative years, it's clear that Nick Woodman's path to success wasn't accidental. Every scraped knee from a bike crash, every wipeout on a surfboard, and every failed attempt at catching the perfect wave on camera was preparing him for his future role as an innovative entrepreneur. His story proves that our earliest experiences and passions often hold the keys to our future success – if we're brave enough to follow them.

As we close this chapter on Nick's early years, we stand at the threshold of his first major business ventures. In the next chapter,

"From Failure to Fortune," we'll explore how these foundational experiences would be tested in the unforgiving world of startups. We'll witness how Nick faced his first significant business failure – a gaming and marketing website called EmpowerAll.com – and how this setback, rather than defeating him, became the catalyst for his future success. We'll see how the lessons learned during his adventurous youth would help him navigate through failure and eventually lead him to the idea that would revolutionize action photography.

The story that follows is not just about business success or technological innovation – it's about the power of resilience, the importance of staying true to one's passions, and the remarkable journey of a young adventurer who refused to let failure define his future. As we move forward, we'll discover how Nick Woodman transformed from a surf-loving entrepreneur into the founder of a company that would change how the world captures and shares its most exciting moments.

2

From Failure to Fortune

In the bright and bustling landscape of late-1990s Silicon Valley, failure wasn't just a possibility – it was practically a rite of passage. But knowing this doesn't make failure any easier to swallow, especially when you're a 24-year-old entrepreneur watching your first company crumble around you. For Nick Woodman, the collapse of his first startup wasn't just a business setback; it was a personal reckoning that would shape his entire approach to entrepreneurship and life.

Fresh out of college in 1997, Nick launched his first venture, EmpowerAll.com, a gaming and marketing platform that aimed to capitalize on the dotcom boom. Fueled by youthful optimism and the seemingly endless possibilities of the internet age, he threw himself into the project with characteristic enthusiasm. The idea was simple enough: create a platform where gamers could win prizes for their achievements. It seemed like a perfect blend of entertainment and marketing, riding the wave of growing internet adoption.

"I thought I had it all figured out," Woodman would later reflect. "I had the energy, the vision, and what I believed was a killer idea. What I didn't have was experience, and more importantly, I didn't know what I didn't know."

The initial months were exhilarating. Nick secured some initial funding, assembled a small team, and began building his dream.

The office atmosphere was electric with possibility, and the long hours felt like stepping stones to inevitable success. He even managed to attract some attention from potential investors who were eager to jump on any internet-related venture during the dotcom bubble.

But as the months wore on, cracks began to appear. The technical challenges proved more complex than anticipated. User acquisition was slower than projected. Investors began asking tougher questions about monetization strategies. The prize-winning mechanism, which seemed straightforward in theory, became a logistical nightmare in practice.

By 1999, EmpowerAll.com was struggling to keep its head above water. Nick found himself in the uncomfortable position of having to lay off employees – people who had believed in his vision and taken a chance on a young entrepreneur's dream. The weight of responsibility felt crushing. "Telling someone they no longer have a job because of decisions you made – that's a kind of pain that stays with you," Nick would later say. "It forces you to question everything about your abilities as a leader and an entrepreneur."

But EmpowerAll.com wasn't Nick's only venture during this period. As if one failing startup wasn't enough, he had simultaneously launched Funbug, another gaming and marketing website that promised to give users a chance to win cash prizes. The idea behind Funbug was similar to EmpowerAll.com but with a refined approach based on lessons learned from his first venture.

However, timing proved to be Funbug's greatest enemy. As the dotcom bubble began to burst in 2000, investors became increasingly skeptical of internet-based businesses, especially those without clear paths to profitability. Despite Nick's best efforts and an investment of over $3.9 million from friends and family, Funbug met the same fate as EmpowerAll.com.

The failure of both ventures wasn't just a professional setback – it was deeply personal. Nick had lost not only his own money but also the investments of people who had trusted him. The weight of this responsibility took a heavy toll on his confidence and self-image.

"I felt like I had let everyone down," he would later admit. "My family, my friends, my employees – everyone who had believed in me. That kind of failure forces you to look in the mirror and ask some really hard questions about yourself."The period following these failures was perhaps the most crucial in Nick's entrepreneurial journey. Instead of retreating from the business world entirely, he chose to process his failures methodically, turning them into lessons that would guide his future endeavors.

First came the practical lessons. The experience taught him the importance of having a tangible product rather than just a concept. He learned that timing in business is crucial – being too early to market can be just as problematic as being too late. Most importantly, he realized that successful businesses need to solve real, concrete problems rather than creating solutions in search of problems.

But the deeper lessons were personal. The failures stripped away any pretense of invincibility and forced Nick to confront his own limitations. He learned that passion alone isn't enough – it needs to be coupled with careful planning, market understanding, and precise execution. The experience also taught him the value of maintaining perspective and finding balance in life.

During this period of reflection, Nick did something that would prove crucial to his future success: he returned to his roots. Instead of immediately jumping into another venture, he took time to reconnect with his passion for surfing and adventure sports.

This wasn't just escape or avoidance – it was a deliberate reset, a chance to clear his head and reconnect with what truly motivated him.

"Sometimes you need to step away from the problem to see the solution," Nick would later explain. "When I was out surfing, I wasn't thinking about business failures or lost money. I was just present in the moment, and that's when clarity started to come back."

This period of reflection and reset was marked by a surprising discovery: failure had made him stronger. The fear of failure, which can paralyze many entrepreneurs, had lost some of its power over him. After all, he had already experienced it, survived it, and was still standing. This realization became incredibly liberating. Nick also began to see how his previous failures had equipped him with valuable skills and insights. He had learned how to build and manage teams, how to pitch to investors, how to handle legal and financial challenges, and perhaps most importantly, how to maintain resilience in the face of adversity. These weren't lessons that could be learned in a classroom – they had to be earned through experience.

During this time, Nick developed what he would later call his "fail forward" philosophy. The idea was simple: every failure contains the seeds of future success if you're willing to learn from it. He began to view his failed ventures not as endpoints but as necessary steps in his entrepreneurial journey.

"The biggest mistake you can make after failing," he would later advise other entrepreneurs, "is to stop trying. The second biggest mistake is to try the same thing again without learning from what went wrong the first time."

This period of introspection and learning was also marked by a significant shift in how Nick approached business ideas. Rather than chasing market trends or trying to create artificial needs, he began focusing on solving real problems that he personally understood. This shift in perspective would prove crucial in his next venture.

As 2001 drew to a close, Nick was a different person from the eager young entrepreneur who had launched EmpowerAll.com. He was humbler, wiser, and paradoxically, more confident – not in his inability to fail, but in his ability to handle failure and keep moving forward.The lessons learned during this period would prove invaluable in the years to come. The habits of careful planning, thorough market research, and maintaining a clear focus on solving real problems would all influence his approach to his next venture. More importantly, the resilience and perseverance developed during these challenging times would provide the foundation for his future success.

As we close this chapter on Nick's early failures, we stand at the cusp of a transformative moment in his journey. In the next chapter, "The Inspiration Behind GoPro," we'll explore how these hard-learned lessons combined with a moment of inspiration during a surf trip to Australia and

Indonesia. We'll see how Nick's understanding of failure and success, combined with his passion for adventure sports, led to an idea that would revolutionize how we capture and share our most exciting moments.

The story that follows isn't just about the birth of a product – it's about how past failures can shape future innovations, and how sometimes the best ideas come not from trying to change the world, but from solving a simple, personal problem. As we move forward, we'll discover how Nick's journey through failure prepared him to recognize and seize an opportunity that would change not just his life, but how millions of people around the world document their adventures.

3

The Inspiration Behind GoPro

They say lightning never strikes twice, but for Nick Woodman, enlightenment struck during a five-month surf trip that would change not only his life but how the world captures its most extraordinary moments. The year was 2002, and Nick had done something that seemed counterintuitive for someone who had just experienced significant business failures – he bought a one-way ticket to Australia and Indonesia, armed with nothing but a surf board, a backpack, and an unrelenting desire to reconnect with his passion.

This wasn't just an escape; it was a deliberate reset. After the collapse of his internet ventures, Nick needed to clear his head and return to what he loved most: surfing. But sometimes, when we stop actively searching for answers, they find us in the most unexpected places.

The Australian leg of his journey started typically enough. Days were spent chasing waves along the coast, meeting fellow surfers, and experiencing the kind of freedom that only comes from being completely removed from the pressures of everyday life. But there was something nagging at Nick's entrepreneurial mind – a persistent frustration that would ultimately lead to his breakthrough moment.

"I wanted to capture my surf sessions, not just for showing off, but to study my technique and improve," Nick would later explain. "But every time I tried to photograph myself or other surfers, the results were disappointing. Either the camera was too risky to use in the water, or the angles were all wrong, or the whole setup was just too cumbersome." This frustration wasn't new – it had been a constant companion throughout his surfing years. But something was different now. Perhaps it was the distance from his previous failures, or maybe it was the clarity that comes from spending hours in the ocean, but Nick began to see this common problem in a new light.

The pivotal moment came during a particularly challenging surf session off the Indonesian coast. As Nick watched fellow surfers struggling with their cameras, trying to capture their moments of triumph on the waves, something clicked. The problem wasn't just his – it was universal among action sports enthusiasts. Everyone wanted to capture their experiences, but no one had created a practical way to do it.

"It was like a light bulb went off," Nick would recall. "I saw all these amazing athletes doing incredible things, but the only people who could see them were the ones physically present on the beach. There had to be a better way."The initial concept was simple: create a wearable camera that would allow athletes to capture their perspective while keeping their hands free for the activity itself. But unlike his previous ventures, this idea wasn't just about spotting a market opportunity – it was about solving a problem he intimately understood.

During quiet evenings in his basic beach accommodation, Nick began sketching out his vision. He wasn't just drawing product designs; he was mapping out a whole new way of capturing and sharing experiences. The camera needed to be waterproof, durable, and simple to use. It had to work in extreme conditions and be affordable enough for the average adventure sports enthusiast.

What made this idea different from his previous ventures was its tangibility. This wasn't an abstract internet concept – it was a physical product that would solve a real problem. More importantly, it was something he would use himself, even if no one else bought it.

The surf trip took on a new dimension. Every session in the water became a research opportunity. Nick observed how surfers moved, what angles would work best for capturing action, and what features would be essential for a camera in these conditions. He talked to fellow athletes, not as a businessman conducting market research, but as a passionate surfer who shared their frustrations.

One particularly memorable conversation happened with an Australian surfer who had rigged up his own camera system using rubber bands and a disposable camera. The makeshift solution was clever but clearly inadequate. This encounter reinforced Nick's belief that there was a genuine need for what he was envisioning.

During his time in Indonesia, Nick experimented with different ways to attach his existing camera to his body. He used rubber bands, modified straps, and various DIY solutions. Most failed spectacularly, but each failure provided valuable insights into what the eventual product would need to be.

"I must have looked crazy," he would later laugh, "paddling out with cameras strapped to my wrist in all sorts of weird configurations. But every time something didn't work, I learned something new about what needed to work."

The vision began to expand beyond just surfing. Nick observed rock climbers struggling to document their ascents, skydivers trying to capture their freefall moments, and mountain bikers attempting to film their trails. The potential applications seemed endless, and each new possibility added fuel to his growing enthusiasm.

What set this idea apart from his previous ventures was its organic nature. This wasn't about chasing a trend or trying to capitalize on a market bubble. It was about solving a real problem that he and countless others faced daily. The authenticity of the need made the vision feel different – more grounded, more purposeful.

As his trip progressed, Nick began filling notebooks with designs, features, and potential challenges. He wasn't just dreaming anymore; he was planning. The failures of his past had taught him the importance of thorough preparation, and he was determined not to repeat old mistakes.

One crucial insight that emerged during this period was the importance of community. Nick realized that success wouldn't just come from creating a great product – it would come from building a community of users who shared the same passion for capturing and sharing their adventures.

"I started imagining this ecosystem of adventure enthusiasts all capturing and sharing their experiences," Nick would later say. "It wasn't just about the camera anymore – it was about enabling people to share their lives in a way that wasn't possible before."The trip also helped Nick understand the importance of authenticity in business. His previous ventures had been about creating artificial experiences, but this idea was about enhancing real ones. The difference was profound, and it gave him a confidence he hadn't felt before.As his time in Australia and Indonesia drew to a close, Nick had more than just an idea – he had a mission. He wanted to create a tool that would help people capture and share their most exciting moments, not just for others to see, but for themselves to relive and remember.

The journey back home was filled with a different kind of energy than the one that had taken him away. Instead of escaping from failure, he was rushing toward possibility. His notebooks were filled with sketches, his mind was clear, and his purpose was defined.But having a great idea was just the beginning. Nick knew from his previous experiences that execution would be everything. He would need to figure out how to turn his vision into reality, and this time, he was determined to do it right.

The surf trip that had started as an escape had become a transformation. Nick had arrived as a failed entrepreneur looking for direction; he was returning as a visionary with a clear purpose. The waves that had helped clear his head had also helped birth an idea that would revolutionize how people capture their adventures.

As we close this chapter on the birth of the GoPro concept, we stand at the beginning of an even more challenging journey. In the next chapter, "Building from Scratch," we'll explore how Nick turned his vision into reality. We'll see the painstaking process of creating the first prototype, the challenges of securing funding while living out of his 1971 VW Bus, and the determination it took to bring the first GoPro camera to market.

The story that follows is not just about product development – it's about the grit and perseverance required to turn an inspired idea into a tangible reality. As we move forward, we'll witness how Nick's passion, combined with the lessons learned from his past failures, helped him navigate the countless challenges of building a revolutionary product from the ground up.

4

Building from Scratch

When Nick Woodman returned from his transformative surf trip in 2002, he wasn't just carrying a dream – he was harboring an obsession. With $30,000 borrowed from his mother and a space in his 1971 VW van that would become both his office and home, he began the grueling journey of turning his vision into reality.

The early days were far from glamorous. Nick's "office" consisted of whatever space he could find in his van, which he parked along the California coast. His desk was often a surfboard balanced across his lap, and his business attire consisted of a wetsuit and board shorts. But what he lacked in conventional resources, he made up for in determination and focus.

"I lived on cup noodles and peanut butter sandwiches," Nick would later recall. "Every dollar I had went into developing the camera. People thought I was crazy, living in a van at 26 when I could have been starting a 'real' career, but I knew this was my shot at redemption."

The first challenge was creating a prototype. Nick had no background in camera technology or product design, but he had something equally valuable – a clear understanding of what the product needed to do. He spent countless hours researching existing cameras, waterproof casings, and wrist straps. His van became a mobile laboratory of sorts, filled with dismantled cameras and sketches of possible designs.

The initial concept was relatively simple: create a wearable, waterproof camera that could capture high-quality photos during intense activities. But as anyone who's ever built anything knows, 'simple' doesn't mean 'easy.' Every component presented its own set of challenges.

Nick's first prototype was essentially a Kodak 35mm camera modified with a custom-built waterproof housing and a rubber band as a wrist strap. It was crude, but it worked well enough to prove the concept. However, the road from working prototype to marketable product was longer and more complex than he had anticipated.

One of the biggest early challenges was finding manufacturers willing to work with an unknown entrepreneur with limited capital. Nick spent months reaching out to various manufacturers, most of whom wouldn't even return his calls. He eventually found a small factory in China willing to take a chance on his idea, but communication was difficult, and the initial samples were far from perfect."Every sample that came back wrong was like a punch in the gut," Nick would later share. "But each failure taught us something new about what needed to be different. We couldn't afford to get discouraged – we just had to keep pushing forward."The development process was a constant cycle of trial and error. Nick would test prototypes in the surf, identify problems, make modifications, and start again. His surfing sessions became product testing opportunities, and every wipeout was a chance to evaluate the camera's durability.

Financial constraints meant Nick had to be incredibly resourceful. He couldn't afford professional product designers, so he learned 3D modeling software himself, often staying up late into the night watching tutorials on his laptop in his van. He couldn't hire a marketing team, so he became his own brand strategist, crafting the company's identity between surf sessions.

One particularly challenging aspect was the waterproof housing. Early versions would leak or fog up, rendering the camera useless. Nick spent weeks testing different materials and designs, often in the cold Pacific waters. Each failure meant another round of modifications and another dip into his dwindling funds.

The stress was immense. Nick's previous business failures weighed heavily on his mind, and the pressure to succeed this time was enormous. He had borrowed money from family again, and the thought of failing them twice was almost unbearable. But this time was different – he wasn't just chasing a market opportunity; he was solving a problem he truly understood.A breakthrough came when Nick realized he needed to shift his focus from creating a perfect camera to creating a perfect housing system. The camera itself could be relatively simple, but the housing needed to be bombproof. This insight led to the development of the now-iconic GoPro case design.

By 2004, after countless prototypes and refinements, the first GoPro Hero was ready for production. It was a simple 35mm film camera in a waterproof housing, attached to a rubber strap that could be worn on the wrist. It was far from the sophisticated digital cameras GoPro would later produce, but it worked, and it solved a real problem.

The initial production run was just 100 units. Nick had to beg and borrow to finance even this small batch, and the stakes were incredibly high. If these didn't sell, there wouldn't be money for a second run. He packed and shipped every unit himself, often working late into the night in his van or his mother's house.

Marketing was another challenge entirely. With no budget for traditional advertising, Nick had to get creative. He attended surf shows and action sports events, demonstrating the camera himself. He would approach professional athletes and offer them cameras to use, hoping to build word-of-mouth buzz.

"I must have looked like a crazy person," he would later laugh, "running around surf competitions with cameras strapped to every part of my body, trying to show anyone who would listen how they worked. But when people saw the footage, their eyes would light up. That's when I knew we were onto something."

The production challenges weren't over once sales began. Quality control issues, shipping delays, and customer service demands all had to be managed with minimal resources. Nick handled everything himself, from answering customer emails to processing returns. Each problem solved was a lesson learned, and each lesson helped build a stronger foundation for the company.

One of the most critical decisions during this period was maintaining control over the company's direction. Despite numerous offers from investors who wanted to take over or redirect the company's focus, Nick remained committed to his original vision. He knew that maintaining authenticity was crucial for the brand's long-term success.

By the end of 2004, GoPro had sold its first thousand units. It wasn't a huge number by industry standards, but it was enough to prove the concept and generate the capital needed for the next production run. More importantly, it validated Nick's belief that there was a real market for his product.

The challenges of building GoPro from scratch had transformed Nick. The experience had taught him patience, persistence, and the importance of staying true to his vision. He had learned to trust his instincts while remaining open to feedback and adaptation.

Living in his van during this period wasn't just about saving money – it was about maintaining focus. Every aspect of his life was dedicated to making GoPro succeed. This single-minded determination would prove crucial in the company's early years."Looking back," Nick would later reflect, "those early days were some of the most challenging but also the most rewarding. When you're building something from nothing, every small victory feels enormous, and every setback teaches you something valuable."

As we close this chapter on GoPro's building phase, we stand at the threshold of the company's first major breakthrough. In the next chapter, "GoPro's Breakthrough," we'll explore how the company transitioned from a small, niche product to a global phenomenon. We'll see how Nick's persistence paid off as GoPro began to gain traction in the market, attract attention from major retailers, and build a loyal following among adventure sports enthusiasts.

The story that follows isn't just about business success – it's about how dedication, authenticity, and a relentless focus on solving a real problem can lead to revolutionary changes in an industry. As we move forward, we'll witness how GoPro's early struggles laid the groundwork for its eventual transformation into a cultural icon that would change how people capture and share their most exciting moments.

5

GoPro's Breakthrough

The tipping point for GoPro didn't come with a bang, but with a wave – specifically, a perfect barrel wave at Pipeline in Hawaii, captured from an angle that had never been seen before. It was 2005, and a professional surfer had mounted a GoPro to his board, recording footage that would change action sports photography forever. When the video started circulating in surf shops and online forums, something extraordinary happened: people didn't just want to watch it – they wanted to know how they could create their own.

This moment marked the beginning of GoPro's transformation from a niche surf photography tool to a global phenomenon. But the road to this breakthrough was paved with countless small victories and strategic decisions that Nick Woodman and his growing team navigated with both precision and passion.

By 2005, the original GoPro Hero was already showing promise in the surf community, but Nick knew that to truly break through, the company needed to evolve. The transition from film to digital was becoming inevitable, and customer feedback consistently pointed toward the need for video capabilities. It was time for GoPro to make its next big leap.

"We were selling enough cameras to survive," Nick would later recall, "but I knew we were just scratching the surface. Our customers weren't just buying cameras –

they were buying the ability to share their stories. We needed to make that easier and better."

The development of the Digital Hero marked a crucial turning point. Released in 2006, it was GoPro's first digital camera, capable of capturing both photos and 10-second video clips. While primitive by today's standards, it represented a massive leap forward in functionality and ease of use. More importantly, it arrived just as social media platforms were beginning to embrace video content.The timing couldn't have been better. YouTube was gaining popularity, and action sports enthusiasts finally had a platform to share their footage. GoPro videos started appearing online, showcasing perspectives that had never been seen before: inside the barrel of a wave, mounted on motorcycle helmets, attached to snowboard rails. Each video served as a powerful advertisement for what the camera could do.Retail breakthrough came in an unexpected way. During a trade show in 2007, a buyer from a major sports retailer happened to walk by GoPro's modest booth. What caught his attention wasn't just the product, but the crowd gathered around watching footage captured by the cameras. Within months, GoPro had its first major retail deal, and the cameras were being stocked in sports stores across the country.

"That first big retail order was terrifying and exciting," Nick would share. "We had to scale up production significantly, and there were so many ways it could go wrong. But we knew this was our shot at the big time."

The company's growth during this period was explosive. Revenue jumped from $350,000 in 2006 to $3.4 million in 2008. But what made GoPro's breakthrough truly remarkable wasn't just the numbers – it was the way the camera was fundamentally changing how people captured and shared their experiences.

Athletes who could never afford professional film crews were suddenly able to document their performances from entirely new angles. Amateur adventurers could share their experiences with the world. The democratization of action photography was underway, and GoPro was leading the charge.

Innovation continued at a breakneck pace. The introduction of the HD Hero in 2009 was a game-changer, bringing high-definition video capabilities to the masses. The footage quality was so impressive that professional filmmakers and television producers began incorporating GoPro shots into their productions.

But perhaps the most significant breakthrough wasn't technological – it was cultural. GoPro wasn't just selling cameras; it was fostering a community. Users began sharing their "GoPro moments" online, creating a viral marketing effect that no advertising budget could match.

"We realized we weren't in the camera business," Nick would explain. "We were in the business of helping people capture and share their passions. That realization changed everything about how we approached growth."

The breakthrough period wasn't without its challenges. Growing pains included supply chain issues, quality control challenges, and the constant pressure to innovate faster than competitors who were beginning to take notice of GoPro's success. But Nick's experience with failure had taught him how to navigate challenges while keeping focused on the bigger picture.

One particular challenge turned into an unexpected opportunity. When customers began requesting better mounting options for their cameras, GoPro developed what would become its now-famous mounting system. This modular approach allowed users to attach their cameras to virtually anything, expanding the possible uses far beyond what even Nick had initially imagined.

Social media played a crucial role in GoPro's breakthrough. The company's YouTube channel became a phenomenon in its own right, featuring spectacular user-generated content that showcased both the camera's capabilities and the amazing things people were doing with it. Each viral video served as a powerful testament to what was possible with a GoPro.

By 2010, GoPro had become more than just a camera company – it was a movement. Revenue had soared to $64 million, and the cameras were being used in ways that nobody had anticipated. From scientific research to military applications, from wildlife photography to family vacations, GoPro was everywhere.The company's success attracted attention from investors, but Nick was careful about who he let in. Having learned from his previous ventures, he maintained control over the company's direction, ensuring that growth didn't come at the expense of the brand's authenticity.

"We had plenty of offers from people who wanted to 'help' us grow faster," Nick would later say. "But we knew that sustainable growth had to come from staying true to our core mission – helping people capture and share their lives in ways they never could before."The breakthrough period was characterized by a virtuous cycle: every new user became a potential content creator, every piece of content served as marketing, and every viral video inspired more people to join the GoPro community. The company had achieved something rare in business – organic, sustainable growth driven by genuine user enthusiasm.

Professional athletes and celebrities began using GoPros not just because they were paid to, but because the cameras offered capabilities that no other device could match. When Felix Baumgartner made his record-breaking space jump in 2012, he had five GoPro cameras mounted on his suit, providing unprecedented views of the historic moment.

The breakthrough wasn't just about selling cameras – it was about changing how people viewed the world around them. GoPro had created a new visual language, a way of capturing moments that made viewers feel like they were part of the action.

As we close this chapter on GoPro's breakthrough period, we stand at the beginning of the company's evolution into a global brand. In the next chapter, "A Brand for Adventurers," we'll explore how GoPro transformed from a successful product into a cultural phenomenon. We'll see how Nick Woodman and his team built a brand that represented more than just cameras – it represented a lifestyle, an attitude, and a new way of seeing the world.

The story that follows isn't just about marketing or brand building – it's about how authenticity, community, and shared passion can create something much bigger than a product. As we move forward, we'll discover how GoPro became not just a camera company, but a symbol of adventure, creativity, and the human desire to capture and share our most exciting moments.

6

A Brand for Adventurers

In the world of business, there's a profound difference between building a product and creating a movement. By 2010, GoPro had proven itself as a revolutionary camera, but Nick Woodman had bigger dreams. He didn't just want to sell cameras – he wanted to inspire people to live bigger, bolder lives and capture their experiences in ways that had never been possible before.

"A camera is just a tool," Nick would often say. "What matters is what people do with it. We're not selling cameras – we're selling the ability to share your passion with the world."

This philosophy became the cornerstone of GoPro's transformation from a successful product into a global lifestyle brand. The journey began with a simple observation: GoPro users weren't just customers; they were storytellers, adventurers, and creators. Each person who strapped on a GoPro became part of a larger narrative about living life to its fullest.The brand-building process started from within. Nick fostered a company culture that embodied the adventurous spirit he wanted GoPro to represent. The company's offices became a hub of activity where employees were encouraged to pursue their own adventures and share their stories. Staff meetings might include footage from someone's weekend surfing trip or a morning mountain bike ride.

"If we're going to inspire people to live adventurously, we need to live it ourselves," Nick would tell his team. This authenticity became GoPro's secret weapon in building a brand that resonated with millions.

The company's marketing strategy was revolutionary in its simplicity: let the users tell the story. Instead of creating polished advertisements, GoPro built its brand largely through user-generated content. The best videos weren't coming from marketing professionals – they were coming from ordinary people doing extraordinary things.

This approach led to the creation of GoPro's iconic YouTube channel, which became a phenomenon in its own right. The channel wasn't just about showing what the camera could do – it was about showcasing the amazing things people were doing with it.

From heart-stopping ski runs to tender moments between parents and children, each video added another layer to the brand's identity.

"Be a Hero" became more than just a tagline – it became a call to action. The message wasn't about being a superhero or a professional athlete; it was about being the hero of your own story, whatever that meant to you. This inclusive approach helped GoPro transcend its origins in extreme sports and connect with a much broader audience.

The brand's visual identity evolved during this period as well. The distinctive GoPro logo and the now-famous camera beep became instantly recognizable symbols of adventure. Even the camera's design, with its minimalist aesthetic and rugged housing, communicated something about the brand's values: simplicity, durability, and readiness for anything.

One of the most powerful aspects of GoPro's brand building was its ability to create a sense of community. The company launched GoPro Awards, a program that rewarded users for sharing their best content. This not only generated a constant stream of amazing footage but also made users feel like they were part of something bigger than themselves.

"Every time someone shares a GoPro video, they're not just sharing their experience – they're inspiring others to go out and create their own adventures," Nick would explain. This viral cycle of inspiration and creation became self-perpetuating, with each new video adding to the brand's momentum.

The company's presence at events evolved from simple product demonstrations to full-blown experiences. GoPro began sponsoring athletes and events across multiple disciplines, but always with the same approach: focus on the story, not the sell. The company's booth at trade shows became known as a place where people could connect with fellow adventurers and share their experiences.Social media played a crucial role in building the brand. GoPro's Instagram account became a daily source of inspiration for millions, featuring a mix of professional athlete content and submissions from everyday users. The democratization of amazing footage meant that anyone could have their moment in the spotlight.

But perhaps the most remarkable aspect of GoPro's brand building was its ability to expand beyond its original market while maintaining its core identity. What started as a tool for surfers and skaters became equally popular among families, travelers, and even professional filmmakers. The brand grew without diluting its essence.

"We never wanted to be just an extreme sports brand," Nick would later reflect. "We wanted to be a brand that celebrates life's incredible moments, whether that's skiing down a mountain or a baby's first steps. What matters is the authenticity of the moment."The company's partnerships reflected this broader vision. Collaborations with everyone from Red Bull to the NHL helped position GoPro as more than just a camera – it was a new way of seeing the world. These partnerships were carefully chosen to align with the brand's values of authenticity and adventure.Education became another powerful brand-building tool. GoPro created tutorials and tips for users, helping them capture better footage and tell better stories. This commitment to user success strengthened the bond between the brand and its community.The company's retail presence evolved as well. Instead of simply placing cameras on shelves, GoPro created immersive displays that told stories and inspired adventures. Video walls showing user-generated content became a common sight in stores, turning point-of-sale locations into points of inspiration.

Corporate responsibility also played a role in building the brand. GoPro for a Cause was launched, using the company's technology and platform to support nonprofit organizations and shine a light on important issues. This demonstrated that adventure could be about more than just personal achievement – it could be about making a difference in the world.

The brand's influence began to extend into unexpected areas. Scientists used GoPros to study marine life, teachers used them to make lessons more engaging, and doctors used them to improve surgical techniques. Each new application added another dimension to the brand's story.

"What amazes me," Nick would say, "is how people keep finding new ways to use our cameras. Every time we think we've seen it all, someone comes up with something completely new and unexpected."

By 2013, GoPro had become more than just a successful company – it was a cultural phenomenon. The brand had tapped into something fundamental about human nature: the desire to capture and share our experiences, to prove we were there, to show others what we saw and felt.

As we close this chapter on GoPro's brand building, we stand at the edge of another transformation. In the next chapter, "Innovation and Evolution," we'll explore how GoPro continued to push the boundaries of what was possible, both technologically and creatively. We'll see how the company adapted to changing market conditions, embraced new technologies, and continued to innovate while staying true to its core mission.

The story that follows isn't just about product development or technological advancement – it's about how a brand built on authenticity and passion continues to evolve while maintaining its connection to the community that helped build it. As we move forward, we'll discover how GoPro's commitment to innovation helped it stay ahead in a rapidly changing market while never losing sight of what made it special in the first place: the ability to help people capture and share life's most meaningful moments.

7

Innovation and Evolution

As the mid-2000s unfolded, GoPro's trajectory wasn't just about maintaining success – it was about redefining what was possible in action camera technology. Under Nick Woodman's leadership, GoPro embarked on a remarkable journey of innovation that would transform a simple wearable camera into a sophisticated ecosystem of products that changed how people capture their lives.

The story of GoPro's evolution begins with the humble Digital HERO, released in 2006. This first digital iteration of the GoPro camera, though basic by today's standards, represented a crucial leap forward. Woodman knew that digital technology was the future, but he also understood that the transition needed to maintain the rugged reliability that had made GoPro famous. The Digital HERO's 3-megapixel sensor and compact design proved that professional-quality digital imaging could be both durable and accessible.

What followed was a period of rapid innovation that would cement GoPro's position as the leader in action cameras. The introduction of the HD HERO in 2009 marked a watershed moment. Suddenly, users could capture stunning 1080p video, transforming amateur footage into broadcast-quality content. Woodman's insistence on pushing technological boundaries paid off – professionals began adopting GoPro cameras alongside enthusiasts, expanding the brand's reach far beyond its action sports roots.

But Woodman's vision extended beyond mere image quality. He recognized that versatility would be key to GoPro's continued success. The development of the innovative mounting system, which became one of GoPro's most significant competitive advantages, allowed users to capture perspectives that were previously impossible. From helmet mounts for snowboarders to chest harnesses for mountain bikers, and even specialized rigs for automotive and aviation use, GoPro created a solution for every adventure.

The HERO2, released in 2011, brought another leap forward with improved low-light performance and sharper image quality. But perhaps more importantly, it introduced WiFi connectivity through the WiFi BacPac accessory. This seemingly simple addition opened up new possibilities for remote control and instant sharing – features that would become increasingly crucial in an increasingly connected world.

Woodman's team didn't stop there. The HERO3 series, launched in 2012, represented a complete redesign. The cameras became 30% smaller and 25% lighter while significantly improving image quality. The HERO3 Black Edition could shoot 4K video, albeit at a modest 15 frames per second, but it signaled GoPro's commitment to staying ahead of the technological curve. The improved WiFi capabilities and the introduction of the GoPro app created a seamless connection between camera and smartphone, making it easier than ever to share adventures instantly.

The evolution of GoPro's product line wasn't just about adding features – it was about solving real problems faced by users. The introduction of SuperView mode offered a wider field of view, perfect for capturing immersive action shots. HyperSmooth stabilization, which debuted with later models, effectively eliminated shaky footage, solving one of the biggest challenges in action photography. These innovations weren't just technical achievements; they were direct responses to user feedback and needs.

2014 saw the release of the HERO4, which brought 4K video at 30fps and improved low-light performance. But more importantly, it introduced Professional Mode, giving serious filmmakers manual control over color, ISO limit, and exposure. This feature demonstrated GoPro's growing ambition to serve not just adventure enthusiasts but also professional content creators.The company's innovation wasn't limited to cameras alone. The launch of GoPro Studio, free editing software designed specifically for GoPro footage, helped users create professional-looking videos without expensive editing tools. The development of the Karma drone, though ultimately discontinued, showed Woodman's willingness to take bold risks and explore new territories.

Throughout this period of rapid innovation, Woodman maintained his hands-on approach to product development. He continued to test prototypes personally, often during his own adventures. This direct connection to the user experience helped ensure that every new feature and improvement served a real purpose rather than just adding complexity.

GoPro's commitment to backward compatibility also proved crucial. New mounts and accessories were designed to work with older cameras, protecting users' investments and building brand loyalty. This approach helped create a sustainable ecosystem where users could gradually upgrade their equipment while maintaining access to their existing accessories.

The introduction of the GoPro HERO5 marked another significant milestone, introducing voice control and GPS capabilities. These features reflected a broader trend toward making technology more intuitive and user-friendly. The addition of water resistance without a separate housing showed GoPro's attention to user convenience while maintaining the durability that had become synonymous with the brand.

As competition in the action camera market intensified, GoPro's pace of innovation accelerated. Each new generation of cameras brought significant improvements in image quality, battery life, and ease of use. The introduction of features like TimeWarp and SuperPhoto demonstrated GoPro's ability to combine technical innovation with creative tools that inspired users to push their creative boundaries.

Nick Woodman's philosophy throughout this period remained consistent: innovation should serve the user's needs rather than just chase specifications. This approach helped GoPro maintain its leadership position even as larger companies entered the market. By focusing on the real-world applications of new technology, GoPro continued to create products that resonated with its core audience while attracting new users.

Looking ahead to Chapter 8, "The Power of Social Media," we'll explore how GoPro's technological innovations dovetailed perfectly with the rise of social platforms. The ability to capture high-quality action footage and share it instantly created a perfect storm of viral content that would take GoPro from a camera company to a global media phenomenon. We'll see how user-generated content became the driving force behind GoPro's marketing strategy, and how the company built one of the most engaged online communities in the tech world. The next chapter reveals how GoPro's innovative technology combined with social media to create a content revolution that would influence how people share their adventures worldwide.

This journey of innovation and evolution demonstrates more than just technical progress – it shows how a clear vision, combined with relentless dedication to improvement, can keep a company at the forefront of its industry. Through continuous innovation and careful attention to user needs, GoPro transformed from a simple camera maker into a global technology leader, forever changing how we capture and share our most exciting moments.

8

The Power of Social Media

In the fast-paced world of social media, few brands have managed to harness its power quite like GoPro. What began as a camera company transformed into a global content phenomenon, creating one of the most engaging and authentic brand communities in the digital age. This is the story of how GoPro didn't just ride the social media wave – they helped create it.

The social media revolution at GoPro began almost by accident. Around 2009, as users started posting their GoPro footage online, something magical happened. These weren't just ordinary videos – they were extraordinary perspectives of life's most exciting moments, captured in ways that had never been seen before. From surfers riding inside the barrel of waves to skydivers capturing their free-fall experiences, GoPro users were creating content that was inherently shareable.

Nick Woodman recognized this organic momentum early on. "We realized we weren't just selling cameras," he would later reflect. "We were enabling people to capture and share their lives in ways that were previously impossible. Our users were becoming content creators, and their stories were our story."

This realization led to a pivotal shift in GoPro's marketing strategy. Instead of focusing solely on traditional advertising, the company began to leverage user-generated content (UGC) as its primary marketing tool.

The company started featuring customer videos on its social media channels, creating a virtuous cycle: the more amazing content they shared, the more people wanted to create their own GoPro moments.

YouTube became GoPro's first major social media success story. The company's channel grew exponentially, eventually becoming one of the most subscribed-to brands on the platform. What made this growth particularly remarkable was that the vast majority of content wasn't created by GoPro – it was created by their users. The company simply curated and showcased the best submissions, turning their YouTube channel into a celebration of human achievement and adventure.

Instagram provided another perfect platform for GoPro's visual storytelling approach. The company's Instagram strategy was brilliantly simple: repost the most stunning photos and videos from their community, always crediting the original creator. This approach not only provided a constant stream of fresh content but also incentivized users to tag their GoPro content in hopes of being featured.

The introduction of GoPro Awards in 2015 took this engagement to the next level. The program offered cash rewards for the best user-submitted photos and videos, turning content creation into a potential source of income for skilled creators. This move helped cultivate a community of semi-professional GoPro content creators who consistently pushed the boundaries of what was possible with the cameras.But perhaps the most brilliant aspect of GoPro's social media strategy was how it transcended traditional demographic boundaries. Their content appealed to everyone from extreme sports athletes to parents capturing their children's first steps. The common thread was authenticity – these weren't polished advertising productions but real moments captured by real people.

The company's hashtag strategy proved particularly effective. #GoPro became more than just a brand marker – it became a symbol of adventure and authenticity. When users tagged their content with #GoPro, they weren't just identifying the camera they used; they were associating themselves with a lifestyle and a community.GoPro's social media success wasn't just about quantity – it was about quality engagement. The company maintained an active presence in their community, responding to comments, offering technical support, and creating genuine connections with their users. This two-way dialogue helped build brand loyalty and created a sense of belonging among GoPro users.

The company also proved adept at leveraging emerging social media trends. When Instagram Stories launched, GoPro quickly adapted their content strategy to include more behind-the-scenes footage and quick tips. As TikTok gained popularity, they embraced the platform's creative, energetic style with shorter, more dynamic content.Professional athletes and influencers played a crucial role in GoPro's social media strategy, but not in the traditional sponsored content way. Instead of just paying for endorsements, GoPro built genuine partnerships with athletes who authentically used their products. This approach led to some of the most spectacular content in GoPro's history, from Felix Baumgartner's space jump to Kelly Slater's inside-the-wave footage.

The viral nature of GoPro content created a unique marketing advantage. Every spectacular video or photo served as a product demonstration, showing potential customers exactly what they could achieve with a GoPro camera. This organic marketing was incredibly effective – people weren't just buying a camera; they were buying into the possibility of creating their own amazing content.GoPro's social media success also influenced product development. Features like WiFi connectivity and the GoPro app were direct responses to users' desire to share their content more easily. The company understood that in the social media age, the ability to quickly edit and share content was just as important as the ability to capture it.

The community aspect of GoPro's social media presence extended beyond just sharing content. The company created GoPro Community Groups, where users could connect with others who shared their interests, from mountain biking to underwater photography. These groups became valuable resources for tips, tricks, and inspiration, further strengthening the brand's relationship with its users.

As we close this chapter on GoPro's social media triumph, we can see how the company transformed from a hardware manufacturer into a content powerhouse. Their success wasn't just about having the right product at the right time – it was about understanding the fundamental human desire to share experiences and build connections.

Looking ahead to Chapter 9, "The Trials of Success," we'll explore how GoPro's rapid growth and market dominance brought new challenges. From increasing competition to the pressures of being a public company, we'll see how Nick Woodman and his team navigated the complex waters of sustained success. The next chapter reveals the less visible side of GoPro's journey – the internal struggles, market pressures, and strategic decisions that tested the company's resilience and adaptability in ways that no action sport ever could.

9

The Trials of Success

Success, as Nick Woodman would discover, brings its own unique set of challenges. By 2014, GoPro had achieved what many startups only dream of – market dominance, cultural relevance, and a successful IPO that valued the company at nearly $3 billion. Yet this pinnacle moment would mark the beginning of perhaps the most challenging chapter in the company's history.

The story of GoPro's trials begins with its transition from a private to a public company. On June 26, 2014, GoPro began trading on NASDAQ under the symbol "GPRO." The IPO was a resounding success, with shares jumping 31% on the first day.

Nick Woodman, still holding a significant portion of the company's shares, became a billionaire overnight. The media celebrated the story of the surfer-turned-CEO who had built a technology empire from a simple idea.But with this public success came unprecedented scrutiny. Every quarterly earnings report, every product launch, and every strategic decision was now under the microscope of Wall Street analysts and shareholders. The pressure to maintain growth rates and meet market expectations was intense, creating a new kind of stress that Woodman and his team had never experienced before.

"Being a public company is like learning to operate in a completely different environment," Woodman would later reflect. "The metrics that matter to Wall Street aren't always aligned with the long-term vision you have for your company. Finding that balance becomes a daily challenge."

The first major test came in late 2015 when GoPro's stock price began to decline amid concerns about market saturation and competition. The action camera market, which GoPro had essentially created, was becoming increasingly crowded. Competitors, including major technology companies, were launching their own products at lower price points. The company's once-unique value proposition was being challenged from multiple directions.In response to these pressures, GoPro attempted to diversify its product lineup. The launch of the Karma drone in 2016 was meant to open up new markets and revenue streams. However, the project faced significant setbacks. Shortly after its release, some units began experiencing power failures mid-flight, leading to a recall. The incident was a stark reminder that even successful companies can stumble when venturing into new territory.

The drone setback had broader implications than just the immediate financial impact. It raised questions about GoPro's ability to expand beyond its core product line. The company had invested significant resources in the project, and its failure affected both market confidence and internal morale. Woodman faced one of the hardest decisions of his career when he ultimately decided to exit the drone market in early 2018."Sometimes the hardest part of leadership is knowing when to step back from something you've invested in heavily," Woodman would say. "The drone market taught us valuable lessons about focusing on what we do best."Internal challenges accompanied the external pressures. The rapid growth of the company had led to an expansion of the workforce and the addition of multiple layers of management. The startup culture that had driven GoPro's early success was becoming harder to maintain. Decision-making processes became more complex, and the company's ability to respond quickly to market changes was affected.

In 2016, GoPro faced another difficult moment when it had to implement significant layoffs, reducing its workforce by about 15%. For Woodman, who had always prided himself on creating a positive work environment, these decisions were particularly painful. The human cost of corporate restructuring was a sobering reality of leading a public company through challenging times. The competition in the action camera market continued to intensify. Smartphone manufacturers were improving their cameras' capabilities, and some consumers began questioning the need for a dedicated action camera. GoPro found itself fighting not just against direct competitors but against the broader trend of smartphone convergence.

However, these challenges also sparked innovation within GoPro. The company doubled down on its strengths, focusing on developing features that smartphones couldn't match. Advanced stabilization technology, rugged durability, and specialized mounts remained unique selling points. The company also began expanding its software capabilities, recognizing that the future of photography wasn't just about hardware.

The period between 2016 and 2018 was particularly transformative. GoPro underwent a significant restructuring, streamlining its product line and focusing on profitability rather than just growth. The company also rebuilt its go-to-market strategy, improving its direct-to-consumer channels and reducing its reliance on traditional retail.

"Success doesn't mean you stop evolving," Woodman observed. "Sometimes it means you have to evolve even faster to stay ahead."One of the most significant challenges was maintaining innovation while managing costs. The research and development required to stay competitive in the technology sector is expensive, but cutting these investments could lead to losing ground to competitors. Balancing these competing demands required careful strategic planning and sometimes difficult trade-offs.

The COVID-19 pandemic in 2020 brought new challenges but also unexpected opportunities. While traditional retail channels were disrupted, the shift to online sales and direct-to-consumer marketing actually played to some of GoPro's strengths. The company's earlier investments in digital infrastructure and direct sales channels proved prescient.Throughout these trials, Woodman's leadership style evolved. The enthusiastic entrepreneur who had built GoPro through sheer force of will learned to become a more measured corporate leader. He surrounded himself with experienced executives who could help navigate the complexities of running a public company while maintaining the innovative spirit that had made GoPro successful.

"Leadership isn't about having all the answers," Woodman would reflect. "It's about building a team that can find the answers together."

The company's relationship with its community also evolved during this period. While GoPro maintained its strong connection with its core users, it also worked to broaden its appeal. New use cases emerged, from professional filmmaking to remote work applications, showing that the company's products could adapt to changing market needs.Perhaps most importantly, these trials taught GoPro the value of resilience. The company learned to weather market volatility, adapt to changing consumer preferences, and maintain its innovative edge even when facing significant headwinds. The experience of managing success proved in many ways more challenging than achieving it in the first place.

By 2021, GoPro had emerged as a more focused and resilient company. While no longer the high-flying growth stock it had been in 2014, it had found a more sustainable path forward. The company's revenue stabilized, its product line became more focused, and its business model more diversified.

"Success isn't just about reaching the top," Woodman would say. "It's about staying there and continuing to evolve, even when the path forward isn't clear."

Looking ahead to our final chapter, "Legacy and Lasting Impact," we'll explore how these trials and transformations shaped not just GoPro's future but its lasting influence on technology, content creation, and adventure culture. We'll examine how Nick Woodman's journey from surfer to CEO to corporate leader has influenced a new generation of entrepreneurs, and how GoPro's innovations continue to shape how we capture and share our most meaningful moments. The final chapter will reflect on the broader implications of GoPro's success and challenges, and what they tell us about innovation, adaptability, and the enduring power of a simple idea executed with passion and persistence.

10

Legacy and Lasting Impact

Nick Woodman's journey from a passionate surfer to an iconic entrepreneur left an indelible mark on technology and the culture of capturing experiences. Reflecting on his legacy, one sees the story of a visionary who, with grit and a deep love for adventure, transformed the way the world documents memories. GoPro wasn't just a camera; it was a way for people to capture life from a new perspective. Woodman's drive to create a camera that could keep up with life's most intense moments brought storytelling tools to thrill-seekers, artists, athletes, and ordinary individuals alike.

In a world where technology often feels distant, Woodman managed to build a product that felt deeply personal. GoPro didn't just record; it empowered people to share, to create, and to connect. People from all walks of life could now document their experiences with a quality that rivaled professional setups, opening doors to endless creative possibilities. The brand became a gateway to telling stories that, in the past, might have gone unnoticed or unrecorded. GoPro found its place not only in extreme sports but also in the daily lives of its users, capturing everything from joyful family moments to breathtaking global journeys.

But Nick Woodman's influence goes beyond technology; he reshaped an industry and even inspired a new mindset around content creation. He believed in breaking down barriers between people and the professional-quality tools required to tell their stories. This vision helped usher in an era where content creation became accessible, relatable, and democratic. Social media platforms blossomed with GoPro videos, sharing perspectives that were once reserved for skilled filmmakers. His innovation empowered individuals, not companies, to own the stage, making everyone a potential storyteller.

This journey wasn't without its share of challenges. Building a brand from the ground up, Woodman encountered tough times, intense competition, and market changes that threatened GoPro's success. As competitors entered the action camera market, GoPro faced the challenge of maintaining its edge. Some questioned the company's ability to keep up as smartphone cameras improved rapidly and competition in the action camera field grew fierce. Through it all, Woodman's resilience stood out. He approached these difficulties with the same adventurous spirit that led him to create GoPro in the first place, always willing to pivot, adapt, and evolve.

One of Woodman's great strengths was his commitment to his original vision, even when it meant making difficult decisions. When GoPro went public in 2014, it opened new opportunities but also added new pressures. The company's rapid growth brought scrutiny and tough business decisions. And while GoPro encountered some stumbling blocks in the public eye, Woodman's determination remained intact. He took setbacks as part of the journey, focusing on refining the product and reimagining GoPro's role in an evolving tech landscape. His resilience became part of his legacy, showing how leaders can face adversity with an open heart and a focus on innovation.

Under Woodman's leadership, GoPro expanded beyond just hardware into the realms of content creation and community-building. He recognized early on the value of the community that had formed around his product, which was especially evident on social media platforms. This became one of GoPro's defining qualities. Instead of relying solely on traditional marketing, GoPro empowered its users to become ambassadors of the brand. By showcasing videos and photos from GoPro users, Woodman built a brand identity that celebrated creativity, authenticity, and adventure. This approach made GoPro more than a product; it became a cultural phenomenon. The GoPro community grew, connecting users globally, fostering a sense of camaraderie, and encouraging people to push boundaries, both physically and creatively.

Woodman's legacy isn't solely about the GoPro product; it's about the attitude he instilled within the brand and its users. His story inspired other entrepreneurs to take bold risks, believe in their visions, and to let passion drive their work. He encouraged others to embrace challenges, viewing them not as setbacks but as stepping stones. Woodman's story resonates with those who aspire to create something meaningful, to bring ideas to life against the odds. His journey serves as a reminder that success isn't about avoiding failure but about learning and adapting along the way. He showed that resilience, creativity, and an unwavering commitment to purpose are the true marks of a visionary.

Today, GoPro's influence is visible far beyond the action sports world. The brand's impact can be seen in how people interact with technology, how they document their lives, and how they share their stories with others. Woodman's commitment to quality, innovation, and the user experience set a high bar in the tech industry. He challenged other companies to prioritize the customer's perspective, emphasizing usability, durability, and versatility. This focus on user-centric design became an inspiration for tech companies worldwide, reminding them that the best products are those that enrich people's lives.

Nick Woodman's journey and the rise of GoPro also highlight the evolving role of technology in self-expression. In many ways, GoPro helped redefine what it means to be an explorer, whether that exploration is of a natural landscape, a bustling city, or one's own backyard. With a GoPro in hand, people felt encouraged to step out of their comfort zones, to see the world differently, and to share those perspectives. Woodman's work exemplifies the idea that technology can deepen our connection with the world and with one another.

Looking forward, Nick Woodman's legacy continues to inspire future creators, innovators, and entrepreneurs. His story is a testament to what can be achieved when passion meets purpose and when one individual dares to challenge the status quo. The action camera market may evolve, and technology will continue to advance, but Woodman's influence on the way we capture and share experiences will endure. Through GoPro, he showed that it's possible to create something extraordinary when you follow your passions wholeheartedly.

In many ways, Woodman's impact has only just begun. The spirit of adventure, creativity, and resilience that he brought to GoPro resonates with new generations who seek to create, connect, and capture life's moments. His legacy is a call to all who dream of building something remarkable: to dare, to innovate, and to inspire. Nick Woodman's story is a reminder that with vision, courage, and dedication, anyone can capture success.

Epilogue

As we conclude the story of Nick Woodman and the rise of GoPro, we are left with more than just the tale of an inventor who turned a simple idea into a global brand. Nick's journey exemplifies the spirit of creativity, resilience, and determination, reminding us that even the most ambitious dreams are possible when driven by passion. His story is an invitation to think beyond conventional limits and to believe that every challenge—no matter how daunting—can be a step toward something greater.

GoPro's success was never just about the camera itself; it was about a new way of seeing the world and sharing those perspectives with others. By bringing professional-grade technology into the hands of everyday people, Woodman sparked a movement that reshaped how we capture and connect over life's moments. He inspired a generation of creators, athletes, adventurers, and visionaries to embrace the power of storytelling, showing that everyone has a story worth sharing.

As technology advances, Nick Woodman's legacy lives on, both in the brand he built and in the countless individuals he inspired to document their lives with authenticity and purpose. His story reminds us that success is never a straight path; it's filled with twists, setbacks, and unexpected turns. Yet, for those who stay true to their vision, who embrace risk, and who refuse to settle, the journey itself becomes as rewarding as the destination.

In the end, Nick Woodman's impact is not only measured in sales, awards, or even technological milestones. His legacy is reflected in the millions of GoPro users who dare to capture life in its rawest form, exploring the world around them and sharing their perspectives. He leaves behind not just a product, but a mindset—one that encourages us to live boldly, dream fearlessly, and capture every moment as it comes.

As we close this book, we carry forward Nick's spirit of adventure and innovation. In doing so, we honor a story that will continue to inspire, reminding us that each of us has the power to capture success, in whatever form that may take.

Acknowledgement

Creating this book would not have been possible without the support, insights, and inspiration from so many individuals who have contributed along the way. First, my deepest gratitude goes to Nick Woodman himself. His relentless passion, resilience, and boundless creativity are the heartbeat of this story, and his openness in sharing his journey allowed us to capture the spirit of GoPro's remarkable rise.

To the GoPro team—past and present—thank you for sharing your stories, your challenges, and your successes. You are the lifeblood of this brand, and your dedication to building and evolving the GoPro community shines through in every product and every adventure captured. I am also grateful to those who took time to recount their personal experiences with GoPro and its impact on their lives and work; your stories brought new depth and perspective to this journey.

A special thanks to my family, friends, and mentors who encouraged me to dive into this project and who have supported me every step of the way. Your faith and encouragement kept me motivated, even in the most challenging moments. Lastly, to the readers of this book—thank you. It's my hope that Nick Woodman's journey, and the legacy he continues to build, will inspire you to pursue your passions boldly and capture your own moments of success.

Thank you, all.

www.ingramcontent.com/pod-product-compliance
Lightning Source LLC
Chambersburg PA
CBHW071520220526
45472CB00003B/1092